the truth about
SPIES
Is James Bond Dead?

by Geraldine & Harold Woods
Illustrated by Norman Nodel

Rourke Enterprises, Inc.
Windermere, Florida 32786

Published by Rourke Enterprises, Inc., P.O. Box 929, Windermere, Florida 32786. Printed in the United States of America.

Library of Congress Cataloging in Publication Data

Woods, Geraldine.
Is James Bond dead?

Summary: Brief biographies of famous spies highlighting their undercover activities.
1. Spies—Biography—Juvenile literature.
[1. Spies] I. Woods, Harold. II. Nodel, Norman, ill. III. Title.
UB270.5.W66 1981 327.1'2'0922 [B] [920] 81-13801
ISBN 0-86592-694-8 AACR2

REAL SPIES

James Bond does not exist. But that has not stopped him from becoming the most famous spy ever. Books and movies of his adventures have thrilled people all over the world.

In James Bond movies there are many surprises. In one, an Italian boatman and an Argentinian cowboy turn out to be Bond in disguise. A dead body in a coffin is really a very much alive gunman, who almost succeeds in shooting James Bond. An ancient monastery proves to be a training center for British agents, who wear monks' robes while practicing karate.

Real spies do not always have such glamorous roles to play. But they do have some things in common with James Bond. Their stories are just as exciting as any Hollywood movie; and they are all masters at seeming to be what they are not.

Rudolf Abel, for example, looked like what he claimed to be — a professional photographer whose hobby was listening to a shortwave radio. He didn't have time, however, to photograph much more than secret documents, and with that radio he ran a Russian spy ring that included two continents. Cicero, on the other hand, really was the lowly servant everyone thought he was. But he had a part-time spying job that earned him over *one million dollars* in less than a year. No one doubted Belle Boyd either, when she pretended to be a proper southern lady. But proper southern ladies do not sit for hours in a closet, eavesdropping on army officers at a secret meeting, or run through a hail of bullets to deliver a message!

Spies have used just about every trick imaginable; and quite a few of these tricksters have been fooled themselves. The stories of Abel, Cicero, Belle Boyd and others, represent just a few of the exciting adventures of real-life spies.

MAJOR MARTIN

April 30, 1943. The Germans and the British were bitter enemies. World War II was nearing its end. On the coast of Spain, which was friendly to the German cause, lay a British submarine. On board was a spy. He was an agent of the British government. In less than twenty-four hours, he would be captured by Spanish officials and turned over to the Germans. This action changed the entire course of the war. The agent was known as William Martin. In his hand was a briefcase full of papers describing an invasion planned by British and American forces. According to these papers, the Allies, as "our side" was called, had chosen Greece as the site of their attack.

There are three interesting things about William Martin and his papers. The papers were filled with lies; the agent's name was not really William Martin; and the agent was not really a spy at all — he was *dead!*

Sicily or Greece?

The story of William Martin and his mission is one of the most incredible in the entire history of espionage. "Operation Mincemeat," as the project was called, began early in 1942. By that time the Germans had lost several important battles in North Africa. However, they still occupied much of mainland Europe. To break Germany's power, the Allies had to invade southern Europe. But where?

After studying the situation carefully, Britain decided that the island of Sicily was the best place to begin. Unfortunately, the Germans were expecting this. British leader, Winston Churchill, was aware that even a fool would know that Sicily was the perfect choice — and Germans were definitely *not* fools. The solution, then, was to lead the Germans to believe that the invasion would take place in another part of Europe. That's when British Intelligence came into the act. Suppose, they said, the Germans were to find some papers saying that Greece, not Sicily, was to be attacked? And suppose those papers also said that a fake attack on Sicily would be made, just to keep the German's attention away from Greece? Such a trick, if it worked, would give the Allies a needed advantage during the battle for Sicily.

A Dead Hero

The whole scheme depended on the Germans' believing that the papers were real. It was especially important that they fall into German hands in a convincing way. If there was even the slightest suspicion that the information was planted, the mission would backfire. The Germans would be even more sure that Sicily was the target.

British Intelligence decided that the best way to get the papers into German hands was to float a corpse to the shore of Spain. The corpse would be made to appear the victim of an air crash. In its hand would be a leather briefcase containing the fake documents. The Spaniards were friendly with the Germans, and could be counted on to pass along any secret documents they found on the body.

But even the body had to be convincing. It had to look as if it had *really* died from drowning. And so "Major Martin" was called into service. During his life, he had been too sick to serve his country. After his death,

however, he was found to be the perfect man for the job. He was just the right age, and he had died of pneumonia. Pneumonia fills the lungs with fluid, just as drowning does. Martin's family was not informed of the details of "Operation Mincemeat." They were simply told that the body was needed for the good of their country. They agreed to give up Major Martin, provided that his real name remain a secret and that he eventually receive a proper burial.

Identity Cards, Theater Tickets, and "Pam"

But finding a suitable body was only part of the job. Major Martin would certainly be well-studied by the Germans. He had to seem real. So British Intelligence went to work creating a personality for the dead man.

What does an average soldier carry around with him? That's what the Intelligence officers asked themselves as they emptied out their own pockets. Letters, identity cards, pictures, house keys — Major Martin had to have all the little odds and ends a normal person accumulates. As Martin's pockets were filled, his personality began to take shape. He had, for instance, recently become engaged. There was a picture of his fiance, Pam, and a bill for her engagement ring. One of the secretaries in the War Office contributed a love letter, signed by Pam. It was well-creased, as if it had been read and re-read many times by a lonely soldier. Martin was also in financial difficulties. A letter from a London bank complained about an overdrawn account. There was a notice that an insurance bill had not been paid, and a stuffy letter from Martin's father, who did not approve of his plans for marriage. Cigarettes, pencil stubs, stamps, and money were added to the collection. London theater tickets for the evening of April 22nd were put in to show when Martin had left London.

Martin's identity card was a real problem. There was no photograph available of the man while he was alive, and pictures of the corpse were not suitable. Even in dim light he quite plainly appeared dead. A proper I.D. photograph had to be found. At last, the Intelligence officers found a live soldier who resembled Martin and took *his* picture.

Finally, the letter stating the reason for the mission was composed. It was signed by a British general named Archie Nye, and addressed to General Harold Alexander, who was serving with American General Dwight D. Eisenhower. The letter was full of references to "Operation Brimstone." It said that during "Operation Brimstone," British forces would invade Greece. American forces would also attack the Italian islands of Corsica and Sardinia. In a master stroke of cunning, the letter also stated that a fake assault on Sicily would be made to draw the German's attention away from the real target.

Optical Instruments

When his papers were completed, Major Martin was prepared for battle. He was dressed in the uniform of the Royal Marines, and packed in a large container of dry ice. On the night of April 17, 1943, the container, which was labelled "Optical Instruments," was taken on board a submarine called the *Seraph.* Thirteen days later, after a brief prayer, the body was lowered into the sea off the coast of Spain. "Operation Mincemeat" was underway. The officers who had planned it for so many months sat back to wait for the results.

They didn't have long to wait. The next morning a message was received in London that the body of a Royal Marine had been picked up by a Spanish fishing boat. To insure the German's interest, the British immediately sent an urgent message to Spain — the marine's briefcase must be recovered! It was, several days later. The envelopes had been carefully resealed, but British Intelligence was sure that they had been opened. Undoubtedly, the Spanish authorities had passed the documents to the Germans, who had photographed them and returned them to the brief-case. The Germans had nibbled at the bait. But had they also swallowed the hook?

The answer came on July 9, 1943, when the Allies invaded Sicily. There were surprisingly few German troops there to oppose them. At the same time, a large concentration of German forces was reported in Greece. It took more than two weeks for Hitler to realize his mistake and order his best general sent to Sicily. He had been in Greece, waiting for an attack that never came! But by that time, it was too late. The Allies captured Sicily, and prepared to invade the mainland. Major Martin had served his country well.

BELLE BOYD

Around the time of the Civil War, well-dressed ladies wore dresses with enormously full skirts. Cinched tightly around the waist, the dresses were worn over petticoats that had stiff, circular hoops. The skirts of Belle Boyd and her friends, however, had more than petticoats underneath! Hanging inside their hoops, like ornaments on a Christmas tree, were weapons. Not one, but many deadly instruments were hidden there — long swords, pistols, and even rifles. Belle and her friends were not trying to defend themselves with these arms. They were trying to help the South win the war.

Martinsburg, the small Virginia town where they lived, was occupied for much of the war by northern troops. But most of the citizens strongly favored the Confederate cause. They often looked for little ways to annoy their northern visitors and help the southern army. Belle Boyd found a great one. She noticed that the Union soldiers hung their weapons in the hallway of an inn while eating a meal. The long swords and oversized pistols used in those days were too uncomfortable to wear while sitting down. As the unsuspecting officers ate, Belle crept into the hallway and grabbed as many weapons as she could. Then she slipped into an empty room and attached the arms to her hoop.

After her first success, Belle enlisted her friends' help in stealing from the soldiers. Soon Union guns and swords were disappearing all over town. Belle arranged for their shipment to the Confederate troops, who always needed such supplies.

Belle's Charms
A Way With Men

Belle also found other ways to help the South. In fact, she became one of the most valuable spies for the Confederate cause. Some of the information she obtained helped the South to win an important battle. Belle was also an unusual spy. Instead of being secretive about her work, as most spies are, Belle was quite open. She seldom used codes, and the notes she wrote — long, detailed descriptions of troop movements and plans for battles — were left lying all over her house. She once even gave an interview about her spying activities to a northern newspaper!

With such publicity, you may be wondering why Belle wasn't imprisoned or shot by the Union army. Actually, she was arrested three times, but each time she was released. The courts seemed to think she was just mischevious and playing at war. They did not understand that she was doing serious damage to the Union cause. Once, after she was caught smuggling information, the judge began to lecture her on her bad conduct — as a father would lecture his child. Belle listened politely. As soon as there was a break in the speech, she bowed her head. "Thank you gentlemen," she said sweetly. Then she turned around and left! No one stopped her, although the judge was undoubtedly planning some sort of punishment.

Belle managed to charm the judge, just as she charmed everyone. She had a lively personality and was a born flirt — she just had a way with men. If the northern officers had known what power Belle's charms had over their men, they would have made conversation with her a crime. Yet she was never unladylike. There is no evidence that her mother, a proper southern matron, ever disapproved of any of Belle's activities. Her main talent seems to have been as a listener. She flashed her sparkling eyes at a Union officer and made him feel as if he were the most interesting man in the world. With such a devoted audience, the soldier would talk, and talk, and talk. Without realizing it, he soon gave away more information than an average troop bulletin.

A Midnight Journey

Belle used her information well. She went to visit her aunt, who lived in a town called Front Royal. Belle's aunt owned a large estate, but the main house had been taken over by Union soldiers. Belle and her aunt were forced to move to a small cottage nearby. Belle quickly became friendly with the young Union officers, especially with one named Captain Kiely. Kiely soon fell in love with Belle. He wrote her poetry and sent her bouquets. She later wrote that he gave her "some withered flowers . . . and a good deal of very important information."

One of the things that Kiely let slip was that a major council of war was going to be held soon in her aunt's house. On the night of the meeting, Belle hid herself in a closet above the room where the officers were sitting. There was a small hole in the floor of the closet. Belle pressed her ear to the hole and lay still until almost one in the morning. When the last Union

soldier had gone to bed, Belle arose and slipped down the stairs. She quickly went to her aunt's cottage and wrote down what she had heard — *all* the plans for movements of the Union army in the area for the next few weeks!

When she finished writing, Belle saddled her horse and rode swiftly to the house where a Confederate army officer was staying. This journey was very dangerous, because there were many Union troops nearby. Belle had a forged travel pass with her, but if seen she probably would have been in trouble anyway. Young southern ladies were not supposed to be galloping around in the middle of the night — epecially with Union battle plans stuffed in their sleeves! This time, Belle was not seen or stopped.

"Kindness of Lieutenant H."

Belle's most famous adventure took place in May of 1862. A major battle was approaching between the southern General Stonewall Jackson and his opponents from the North. Belle needed to go behind Union lines, to Winchester, to pick up some documents. The Union officer in Front Royal, where she was staying, refused to give her the pass required for the journey. But such a small detail didn't trouble Belle. She quickly went to see a northern officer named Hasbrouck.

"You are a friend of mine, aren't you?" she asked. "Prove it by taking me past the sentries."

Hasbrouck hesitated a moment and then agreed. That decision was to cost him his military career. When Belle, Hasbrouck, and Belle's slave, Eliza, arrived in Winchester, Belle said she had some errands to do. She left Hasbrouck and went to the home of a wealthy southern gentleman. He gave her two packages and a note. One package was not important, he explained. It merely contained newspapers. But the other package and the note were of great importance. It was essential that they reach General Stonewall Jackson.

Belle kept the note herself and gave the package of newspapers to Eliza. She casually asked Hasbrouck to hold the important package for her. To encourage the Union soldiers not to check too closely, she had written "Kindness of Lieutenant H." on both packages. ("Kindness of" is an old-fashioned way of saying "in care of".) She hoped the sentries would think the packages belonged to Lieutenant Hasbrouck.

She also sent flowers to the Union commander of Winchester, along with a note asking for a pass to get back to Front Royal. She had managed to get to Winchester without one, but she wanted to take no chances on the way back. The packages she was carrying were too important to risk! Unfortunately, her safety precautions backfired. If Belle needed a pass to get home, reasoned the Union commander, she must have come without one. That was unusual enough for him to do some checking. Sure enough, someone had seen the packages being passed to Belle. The commander, Colonel Fillebrown, had Belle arrested.

Belle, Eliza, and Lieutenant Hasbrouck were taken to headquarters. There, a Union soldier named Beale demanded that Belle produce the papers she was carrying. Hiding the important note in her hand, she gave him the package of newspapers. Lieutenant Hasbrouck, who didn't know that Belle was a spy, saw the words "Kindness of Lieutenant H." on the wrapping. He began to suspect the truth. "Just a moment," he said, "that package is not mine. I don't know why my name is on it." He pulled the other package out of his

jacket. "This is not mine either." As Beale began to undo the knots, one of the guards spied the note in Belle's hand.

"Give me that paper," said Beale.

"This?" asked Belle calmly. She walked slowly toward him, holding the paper in front of her. She was hoping that Beale would think that if she offered the paper to him willingly, it must be unimportant. But she was prepared to pop the paper in her mouth and swallow it if Beale insisted upon seeing it. (In a popular novel of the day, called *The Spy,* that's what the hero did when *he* was arrested. Belle had just read the book.) To Belle's relief the trick worked! Beale, more concerned with punishing Lieutenant Hasbrouck, ignored the paper. He allowed Belle to return to Front Royal! Although she lost the packages, she was able to deliver the note.

Bullets Flew Around Her

Belle arrived in Front Royal just in time. The Confederate forces of General Stonewall Jackson had just begun to attack the Union troops which held the town. She soon found a friendly Union officer.

"What shall we do sir, the rebels are attacking!" cried Belle.

"Don't worry miss, we'll be safe," he replied. "We will fight as long as we can and then retreat to Winchester. We'll burn our supplies and the bridges on the road behind us. When we meet up with General Banks' forces, they'll defend us!"

"I'm so glad," answered Belle. The officer hurried away, never realizing he had given a good summary of the Union's plans to a notorious spy.

Belle wasted no time. She grabbed her bonnet and ran to tell the Confederates what she had learned. Her route took her directly through the battlefield, where bullets flew all around her. In spite of the danger, she arrived safely and delivered her information to a member of Jackson's staff. Because of Belle's help, the southern troops were able to win the battle.

After The War

It seems incredible that Belle could escape capture after all these adventures, but escape she did — for one more year. In June, 1863, she was finally arrested and sent to Old Capital Prison. Even in jail, her famous charm was evident. She became engaged to another prisoner and convinced her guard to buy the wedding clothes! The marriage never took place, and Belle was released and sent south.

A year later, she was a passenger on a boat sailing illegally from Virginia to Europe. The boat was captured by northern sailors, but even that was not enough to bother Belle. She promptly became engaged again — to the Union commander of the boat! She persuaded her fiance to join the Southern cause and eventually the couple reached Europe, where they were married. Belle began a successful stage career. Her adventures as a spy must have provided her with good acting exposure. She played many roles, but none, perhaps, as exciting as her own adventures.

MATA HARI

On a chilly morning at dawn, a small, pretty woman stood alone. It was October 16, 1917. In front of her was a French firing squad. "I am innocent," she had said over and over, during the months of her imprisonment and trial. No one had believed her. Now she stood silent, waiting. The order came to fire, and Mata Hari died.

Mata Hari became the most famous female spy in history. In fact, her name has come to mean just that. If you say, "She's a real Mata Hari," no other explanation is necessary. It is understood that the woman being described is a glamourous spy.

Yet, the incredible thing is that Mata Hari may not have deserved her reputation at all. The woman who kept insisting that she was innocent *may have been telling the truth.* The French, of course, were convinced that Mata Hari was guilty. But many researchers, reading over the facts of the case years later, are not so sure. Mystery still surrounds this famous lady. Was she a German spy, or was she innocent? If she was a spy, exactly why did she start her career in espionage? And how much did she accomplish? All these questions are still being asked about Mata Hari. After reading her story, decide for yourself whether or not you think Mata Hari was, as the man who arrested her said, "a born spy."

A Spirit of Adventure

Mata Hari's real name was Margaretha Zelle. She was born in the little Dutch town of Leeuwarden in 1876. When she was fourteen, her mother died, and Margaretha was sent to live with her uncle's family in a

Dutch city called The Hague. They were kind, but in Margaretha's eyes, boring. The young Dutch girl was sure that she was meant to have a different kind of life — romantic and exciting.

So Margaretha was very interested in the advertisement she saw in the *Amsterdam Daily News* one day in 1895. It read as follows:

OFFICER ON LEAVE FROM THE DUTCH EAST INDIES WISHES TO MEET A SUITABLE YOUNG LADY. OBJECT MATRIMONY. CONTACT ______________________.

The notice contained little information, but that didn't stop Margaretha. Her imagination supplied the details: a lonely and handsome officer, rich no doubt, living in the mysterious East. It was a combination easily dreamed by an eighteen-year-old girl. Whatever she thought, answering the ad took one thing that the future Mata Hari definitely had — a spirit of adventure. Margaretha probably didn't hesitate at all before sitting down to write a letter.

The Mysterious East

We don't know what Margaretha said in her letter, but we do know that Captain MacLeod soon arranged to meet her in a nearby museum. If her dreams had been of a handsome soldier, they did not come true. MacLeod was an ordinary, balding man with a bushy mustache. At thirty-eight, he was over twice her age. Apparently, that didn't bother the young girl. Only a few months later, Margaretha and the Captain were married. They lived in Holland for almost two years. Then the MacLeods, with their infant son Norman, sailed for the East Indies.

Although she talked about it for the rest of her life as a romantic, exciting place, the East was not kind to

Margaretha. A servant, angry with his master, poisoned Norman. Margaretha became sick. The heat and swarms of insects were upsetting. The MacLeod's marriage — never very strong — began to fall apart. By 1902, they gave up and returned to Holland. A few months later, the couple divorced. John MacLeod was awarded custody of their five-year-old daughter, Jeanne-Louise, who had been born in the Indies.

Margaretha was left with no family, no job, and very little money. But she did have some advantages. She had a talent for finding a way out of even the tightest situation. More importantly, her spirit of adventure was still in one piece. At that time, Paris was known to be the most glamourous city in the world. Margaretha traveled to Paris and checked in at the elegant Grand Hotel. She had learned to ride well in the Indies. Soon she convinced a showman to give her a job as a horsewoman in the circus. Eventually, her employer encouraged her to try dancing.

Eye Of The Morning

She was an instant success. Crowds flocked to see the beautiful, young woman who danced in veils and jewelry. She was said to be an Oriental dancer although, of course, she was Dutch, and had made the dances up herself. Musicians wearing turbans surrounded her, perfume filled the air, and the stage was decorated with palm trees and flowers.

Margaretha began to tell romantic stories about her background. She called herself "Lady MacLeod." As she explained to a new American magazine called *Vogue,* she had grown up on an exotic island in the East called the Isle of Marouda. Her grandfather was Regent of the island. She had played as a young girl in many temples of Marouda, learning the sacred dances. At seventeen, she married "Lord MacLeod" and moved with him to Scotland. That's why her name was Lady MacLeod!

But Margaretha also took another name — Mata Hari. She explained that one by saying that she was born in the south of India. Her family belonged to the sacred class called Brahmins, she explained to her admirers. Her mother died the day she was born, said Mata Hari, and the priests of the Temple of Kanda-Swany adopted her. They gave her the name "Mata Hari" which means "Eye of the Morning." They cared for her during her childhood and taught her the sacred dances of India. One day she was carried off by a handsome British officer named MacLeod. When he died, claimed Mata Hari sadly, she came to Europe and began dancing.

There are many other versions of the story Mata Hari told about her past. Besides her talent for riding and dancing, she apparently had a talent for lying. After so many lies, perhaps she even convinced herself that she had a glamorous background. She may have

begun to believe her own stories! However, many of her listeners knew she wasn't telling the truth. Once at a garden party, for example, a lady announced very loudly, "She an Oriental! Don't be silly!" The other guests gasped, but Mata Hari didn't even bother to reply. Because of her stories, she began to build a reputation as one of the worst liars in Paris.

Years later, during her espionage trial, Mata Hari's reputation as a liar proved to be her downfall. But when she was dancing, it did her no harm. Huge audiences came to see her perform. Fashionable ladies hurried to invite her to their homes. Men were also drawn to Mata Hari, and she enjoyed many romances. Soon she was invited to dance all over Europe.

The Countess von Linden

A few years later, Mata Hari took another step that was to lead her to the firing squad. She went to Germany and performed her first act of espionage. Why did she bother to do something as risky as this, when she was already a successful dancer? Of course, we cannot know for sure. But her latest escapade was not that much different in spirit from answering John MacLeod's letter when she was a girl. Only this time, her spirit of adventure led her on a much more dangerous path. Using the name "the Countess von Linden," she romanced a Russian courier and stole the secrets that he was carrying to the Russian ambassador in Paris. At this point, Mata was probably not a professional spy; she may have done it just to see if she could, or as a favor to her many friends who were in high positions in the German government.

In 1914, World War I began. Germany and France became enemies. Mata Hari fled to Holland, and then made her way back to Paris. Because of her stay in Germany, some people were suspicious of her. She was accused of being a spy for Germany. There were rumors that if she waved her fan a certain way, ships would be sunk in the Mediterranean soon after. Seemingly innocent letters she wrote were said to be coded plans for attacking supply ships.

Mata Hari denied the rumors. She had not, she claimed, come back to France to spy for the Germans. Was she telling the truth? Even now, no one really knows for sure. The French Intelligence Agency, however, became suspicious.

A Secret Test

In the summer of 1916, the French picked up Mata Hari up for questioning. She was charming. With tears in her eyes, she faced her accusers. "But Sirs, how can you suspect me of spying for Germany? I am a true French patriot!" The French officials were unsure. Mata Hari *seemed* to be telling the truth. But, after all, she was known to be an excellent liar. So they proposed a secret test for her.

"Madame MacLeod," they said, "we believe you. We are sure you really do love France. We need your help. You are not, as you say, a spy now. But you can become one — for us!" The French then gave her an assignment in Holland. She was to travel there by way of Spain. However, the French did not trust her completely. To see if she was loyal, they had her followed while she was in Spain.

Their suspicions seemed to be justified. While Mata Hari was in Spain, she phoned a German official. No one knows what she said, but just the fact that she made the call made the French believe that Mata Hari was really spying for Germany. When it was time to continue her journey, Mata Hari sailed for Holland. Her boat made a stop in England, and she was picked up for questioning by British Intelligence. "You do not need to worry about me," said Mata Hari. "I *am* a spy — but for your friends, the French." The British officers did not know what to do. They did not have enough evidence to arrest her as a spy, but they did not trust her either. They suggested that instead of completing her mission in Holland, she go back to Spain and wait there until the war was over. The strongest advice they gave her was to stop spying immediately — for either side. If she had done as the British suggested, she probably would have lived much longer.

In Madrid, Mata Hari, calling herself Lady MacLeod again, settled in at the Palace Hotel. She spent a lot of time with Major Kalle, a German soldier, and Colonel Denvignes, a French soldier. She passed some information she had obtained from the German to the

French soldier. But did she also pass French secrets the other way — to the Germans? Was she a double agent? Although they could not prove it, the French Intelligence officials definitely suspected this was true. When she arrived back in Paris in 1917, they must have been tempted to arrest her immediately. But Mata Hari had many friends with important jobs in the French government. The Intelligence officials knew these men would protect her unless solid evidence existed.

Finally, French Intelligence officials broke a secret German code. They intercepted this message: "Agent H21 arrived Madrid, has got herself in the French service. Been returned to Spain by the British. Demands money and instructions." The reply told H21 to return to France and continue spying. Who else could H21 be but Mata Hari? This was the evidence the Intelligence officers needed. It was now beyond doubt, they said, that Mata Hari was a double agent.

On January 13, 1917, Mata Hari was resting in her bedroom. Suddenly several agents rushed in. "You will come with us, H21," they said. She was shocked and upset. She had no choice but to follow their orders. Once in prison, the famous dancer was questioned ruthlessly by Captain Pierre Bouchardon. Unfortunately for her, the captain seems to have been one of the few men *not* to fall for her charms. He paced the room as he spat out question after question at her. She tried to act unconcerned, denying everything. But soon Mata Hari began to show the strain. One day she asked for a glass of water. When she received it, she took a sip and threw the rest on Bouchardon's pants — a terrible breach of etiquette by 1917 standards!

When she saw she was getting nowhere, she tried a different strategy. One morning she came in and announced that she was finally going to tell the truth. "I did not do so before because I was ashamed. But I am still innocent," said Mata Hari tearfully. Bouchardon

was unmoved. "Let me explain," she continued. "When the war began, I was forced to flee Germany quickly. I had to leave my beautiful furs behind. The Germans *did* offer me money to spy for them. I took it because I felt they owed me payment for my furs. Yes, I pretended to be a double agent. But I gave the Germans only useless information in return for their money."

Innocent or Guilty?

Was Mata Hari, the famous liar, finally telling the truth? Again we do not know. She *did* leave Germany quickly — without any furs. And she *did* receive several payments from the Germans. But no one, in the sixty-odd years since her death, has ever been able to prove that she passed secrets to the Germans. She *may* have been a double agent; but she may simply have been *pretending* to be a double agent, just as she had pretended to be an Oriental dancer.

Bouchardon, of course, did not believe her. The French court agreed with him. After a trial that lasted only a day and a half, they sentenced her to death. With Mata Hari, died the solution to this fascinating mystery. We will never know the truth about Mata Hari, the most famous woman spy in history, who may have been innocent after all.

CICERO

One dark night in December, 1943, two men were riding through the streets of Ankara, Turkey. From time to time the driver glanced nervously into the rear-view mirror. In the back seat sat a short man with thick black hair. His pockets were stuffed with wads of British banknotes. The bills — over $30,000 — had been given to him in exchange for a small roll of film.

Suddenly, the driver noticed a limousine half a block behind the car. This was not unusual; but the driver was a cautious man. Keeping a careful eye on the rear-view mirror, he slowed down. The limousine slowed down too! The driver stopped the car. The limousine came to a quick halt also. That was enough for the passenger. "We have to get away," he cried. But the driver, a German Intelligence officer, didn't need to be told. He had already pushed the gas pedal to the floor. The car leapt forward through the dark with the limousine following close behind.

Eighty, ninety, a hundred miles an hour and more — the two cars screeched through the streets of Ankara. But the big limousine was no match for the smaller, more powerful vehicle. The distance between them grew, and the smaller car managed to escape.

When he was certain they were alone, the passenger snapped, "Take me to the British Embassy." As they neared the gates, the car slowed. The passenger jumped out and the driver sped away. The man with pockets full of banknotes sighed with relief as he hurried inside. It had been a close call.

From Servant To Spy

The man who slipped into the British Embassy that December night was named Elyeza Bazna. He was a Turk who spied for the Germans. He was employed by the British, who were fighting the Germans in World War II. Bazna often met his contact, a German Intelligence officer named Moyzisch, in Moyzisch's car. As they drove through the city, Bazna would leave a roll of film on the front seat. The film contained secrets stolen from the British Embassy. In return, he would receive fabulous sums of money.

The men in the limousine were American Intelligence agents. They knew, as did their allies in British Intelligence, that someone was selling information to the Germans. They had tailed Moyzisch hoping to discover the identity of the spy. Unfortunately for the Americans, Bazna escaped to continue a career as strange and exciting as any spy from television or the movies.

Elyeza Banza's career in espionage only lasted a year. During that time, he was paid more than *one million dollars* for his work. Yet he was not a James Bond character who crawled through windows or charmed the general's wife. He was, instead, the lowliest servant in the British Embassy in Ankara. His duties as "valet" to the ambassador included preparing a morning bath for his boss and cleaning his clothes.

Elyeza Bazna came from a proud Turkish family that had fallen on hard times. In his youth, he had had a variety of jobs. Once he worked with a locksmith, which was good training for his future profession! His hobby was photography, which also came in handy later.

In 1942, while Europe was embroiled in World War II, Bazna became a servant in the German Embassy in

Ankara, Turkey. However, the job didn't last long. Bazna was lazy and proud, and considered his master's belongings as his own. He once took a picture of himself lying on the ambassador's sofa! He also photographed the ambassador's mail, just for the fun of it. Because of his snooping, Bazna was fired.

Black And Red Boxes

In April, 1943, Bazna decided to become a spy. During his time at the German Embassy, he had enjoyed sorting through other people's mail and belongings. It made sense, thought Bazna, to get paid for it. He didn't care which side he spied for as long as he made a lot of money. He soon got a job as a driver for the first secretary at the British Embassy, where he decided to steal British secrets and sell them to the Germans. He immediately began to read his employer's secret papers. They were interesting, but not good enough for Bazna. His ambition was to obtain the papers of the ambassador himself. Very soon the job of valet to Ambassador Sir Hughe Knatchbull-Hugessen became vacant. With a little help from a friend, who was also a servant in the secretary's house, he managed to get the job.

Bazna wasted little time in organizing his spy business. The documents in the ambassador's home were kept in black and red boxes. The red boxes were locked in the office safe at night. But the really important papers were left in the black box, which was kept on the night table; so Sir Hughe could read and study them in bed.

As valet, Bazna was often in the ambassador's bedroom alone. The black box was locked, but that was no problem for the former locksmith. He carried a ball of wax in his pockets, waiting for the perfect opportunity. One day, as he was laying out Sir Hughe's clothes, it came. The ambassador usually kept his keys with him when he took his morning bath. This time, however, he forgot and left them on the bedside table. Bazna listened for the splash of Sir Hughe's bath water, and then grabbed the keys. He carefully pressed them into the soft wax. The impressions they left could later be used to make copies of the keys. Bazna then wiped the keys carefully on one of his employer's best silk handkerchiefs, and replaced them on the night table. Just then, Sir Hughe appeared. Bazna covered his confusion by holding the handkerchief up to the light. "This needs to be sent to the laundry," he said. Sir Hughe nodded, picked up his keys, and returned to the bathroom. Bazna later told his friend that the ambassador should not have been so modest. If he had not taken the time to put on his robe, he would have caught Bazna in the act!

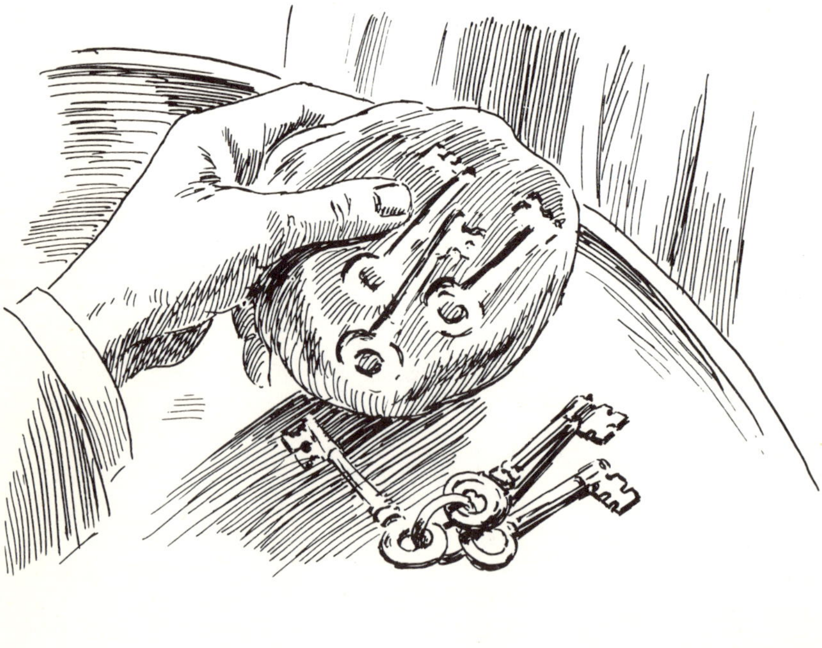

Code Name Cicero

The spy quickly worked out the best method for copying documents. He bought a hundred watt bulb for the reading lamp near his bed. It was a little strong for reading, but fine for lighting the secret papers he wanted to photograph. Four metal rods and a ring were the only other things Bazna needed. They quickly snapped together to form a stand for his camera. He used the rods to hang up his ties and socks when they weren't needed for photography. The ring served as a decoration on Bazna's ashtray.

After his first roll of film was ready, Bazna was able to look for a buyer. He contacted a man named Albert Jenke, who was an official in the German Embassy.

Jenke referred him to a member of Hitler's S.S. group named Moyzisch. Bazna made his offer — two rolls of film showing secret documents for 20,000 British pounds. This was his bargain rate. Additional rolls would be available at 15,000 pounds each.

At first Moyzisch thought Bazna was joking. But when he developed the film he could hardly believe his eyes! The most secret and important papers of the British ambassador were clearly reproduced. Included on the films were the names of all the British agents in Turkey, as well as plans for many secret military operations. Moyzisch quickly gathered 20,000 pounds and gave them to Bazna. To keep his identity a secret, the Germans gave him the code name "Cicero."

In the weeks that followed, Cicero photograhed hundreds of secret documents. He delivered so many rolls of film that sometimes Moyzisch didn't even have enough money to pay him. Cicero told him not to worry — the German government's credit was good! And indeed, the money was always paid eventually. Cicero began to accumulate so many banknotes that he didn't know what to do with them. He was afraid to open a bank account. (A valet doesn't usually deposit over $30,000 a week!) So he spread the money under the rug in his room and walked on his fortune.

Useless and Misleading Information

The secrets that Cicero handed over to the Germans included the date of the famous "D-Day" invasion of France, and plans for a major bombing raid on Sophia, Bulgaria. However, the amazing fact is that the

information was never used. Although one German official trusted Cicero and insisted he be paid, other, more important men did not. Presented with so much top-secret material, the German High Command could not believe it was real. Although the documents Cicero obtained consistently proved accurate, they were placed in a file in Germany marked "Useless and Misleading Information"!

One time, however, the Germans *did* use Cicero's material, and the British quickly realized there was a "leak" in their embassy in Turkey. Cicero laughed as workmen changed the locks on the windows and doors. Although he was taking incredible risks, the only close call he had was when the limousine chased his car. The American agents failed that time. However, both the British and American agents continued to investigate, and finally they discovered who Cicero really was.

The Fortune That Was Not

In April, 1944, Cicero's career ended. He did not have to face a firing squad, as did Mata Hari. Instead he went *free.* Perhaps because the British were embarrassed to have been fooled so easily, they did not even bring Cicero to trial. They simply let him know that he had been discovered. Cicero politely gave notice that he was quitting his job, destroyed his photographic equipment, and left.

But the strange affair known as "Operation Cicero" was not over yet. Bazna rented an expensive apartment and prepared to live a life of luxury. But he soon received a terrible surprise. When he used some of his great stock of British notes to pay a debt, they were returned by the bank. Except for the first few installments, *all the money Cicero had been paid was counterfeit.* The spy who had fooled everyone was, in the end, made a fool of himself.

THE SPY FROM BROOKLYN

On August 2, 1902, a baby named Emil Robert Goldfus was born in New York City. One year and two months later, Emil Goldfus died. In 1950, he was born again. This time, however, he was a middle-aged man — tall, thin, and balding. He lived quietly in Brooklyn, a part of New York City. "Goldfus" worked, he said, as a professional photographer. The new Emil Goldfus, however, was actually a spy who took the identity of the real Emil Goldfus. He was really a colonel in the famous Russian intelligence agency called the KGB.

What, you may be wondering, was a colonel in the KGB doing in Brooklyn? Spies in the movies always seem to live in mysterious foreign capitals or, at the very least, in Washington, D.C. For that matter, why should Russia bother to send a spy here at all? The United States and Russia were not at war. New York City, in fact, was about as peaceful in 1950 as it ever gets. Why should Russia want a spy there?

The answer, of course, is the Cold War. The Cold War was called "cold" because no bombs or guns were used. But it was still a war, because the United States and the Soviet Union were bitter enemies. They opposed each other in every way *except* with arms, in many places around the world. At any time, and without any warning, the "cold war" could heat up; and the Soviet Union intended to be well prepared.

Keeping a spy in Brooklyn, a part of the largest city in the United States, was not that strange an idea. New York is a port city, so a spy there could keep an eye on troop and supply movements. Many businesses, as well as the United Nations, also have their headquarters in New York City. Some, perhaps, had interesting secrets to steal. Moreover, "Goldfus" was not only concerned with New York City. He headed a huge Soviet spy ring. Agents brought him information from all across the United States, Canada, and even Mexico and Central America. From a small apartment in Brooklyn, "Goldfus" transmitted this information to Moscow. He was so successful that even now, twenty-five years later, it is unclear exactly how much secret information "Goldfus" obtained. We do know that he was one of the best spies ever sent to the United States. According to the F.B.I., "Goldfus" was the Master Soviet spy of the twentieth century.

One Person, Many Names

The man who called himself "Emil Goldfus" was born in southern Russia exactly one month earlier than the real Emil Goldfus. No one has ever discovered his real name. He usually claimed it was Rudolf Ivanovich Abel, but many people doubt this because Abel is a favorite alias of KGB agents. Since that is the name he preferred, however, we will call him Abel.

Abel was the only child of a middle class family. He was very intelligent, learning six languages, advanced math, and physics easily. These talents were very helpful to him later in his career in espionage. By the time he was a young man, Abel was teaching English, German, and French in a high school in Moscow. At twenty-five, he joined the Soviet secret police and was assigned to the KGB, in the foreign intelligence section. In the 1930's, as war with Germany approached, Abel's talents were needed. He was sent to the German front and was later decorated for distinguished service to his country. After the war, Abel arrived in Canada. How he got there shows the cleverness of the KGB.

When World War II ended in 1945, there was tremendous confusion in Europe. Thousands of people had fled from the fighting and now had no place to go. Their homes, and in some cases their countries, were destroyed. these people were called "displaced persons" and lived in camps until they could be settled in permanent homes. In the midst of such confusion, the normal records of births and deaths were often lost. It was an ideal time to "plant" people with false identities, and the KGB took full advantage of it.

Abel, using the name Andrew Kayotis, entered a displaced person's camp in Germany in 1946. The *real* Andrew Kayotis was a native of Lithuania, which is a part of the Soviet Union. In 1916 he had moved to the United States and become an American citizen. After World War II, Kayotis was not well. He decided to go home to die. Apparently he did die, in a Lithuanian hospital, just in time for his identity to be used by Rudolf Abel. In 1948, Abel entered Canada with Andrew Kayotis' passport. From Canada, Abel traveled to the United States.

Once inside the United States, Andrew Kayotis became two people — Emil Goldfus and Martin Collins. The spy used two names, making his identity even harder to trace. Abel rented a painter's studio in Brooklyn, under the name of Goldfus, where he kept his spy equipment. He doesn't seem to have worried much about getting caught — the studio was right across the street from the office of the F.B.I.! Martin Collins never existed at all, although Abel had a false birth certificate and other papers in his name supplied by the KGB. Using Collins' name, Abel rented a cheap hotel room in Manhattan to stay in at night. Every day Martin Collins, like thousands of New Yorkers, took the subway to work. Only by the time he got there, his name was Emil Goldfus!

A Crack In The Steps

Now Abel was ready to set up shop as a spy. He quickly contacted all the Russian agents in the area, using still another name — "Mark". Because it was too dangerous to be seen with these men, Abel set up a system of "drops" where information could be sent and received.

The "drops" were amazingly clever. An iron fence, the base of a lamp post, and the bottom of a phone booth seat were among the "mailboxes" Abel used. Hundreds of people walked by these drops every day. Abel and his agents could go there often without making anyone suspicious. Even if someone did find a drop, they were not likely to recognize the message that was left there. A crack in some concrete steps in Brooklyn's Prospect Park, for example, contained a rusty, iron bolt. The bolt, however, unscrewed to reveal a tiny space. A message that was small enough, could easily be tucked inside. Abel hollowed out many other ordinary items, such as pencils, cufflinks, and flashlight batteries, and used them as "envelopes" for his messages.

Only once, in all the years Abel spied in the United States, was one of his secret letters discovered. In June, 1953, a thirteen-year-old boy named Jimmy Bozart was collecting money for his paper route. At one of his stops, Jimmy received a handful of change from a customer. As he walked down the stairs, Jimmy tripped and dropped a coin. To his amazement, it split in half! A tiny piece of film was inside. Jimmy turned the coin over to the F.B.I. They magnified the film and found a coded message which no one was able to understand. The F.B.I. knew there was a spy operating in Brooklyn. The woman who gave Jimmy the nickel was cleared of any wrong-doing. But she couldn't remember where she had gotten the coin. F.B.I. agents

questioned people all over the neighborhood, but they couldn't find the man who made the nickel.

To make sure his messages were small enough for his containers, Abel also set up a photographic studio. In a course in "spy photography" back in Moscow, Abel had learned how to make microdots. A microdot is a very small picture. If this page were made into a microdot, it could fit on the period at the end of this this sentence. Abel also learned how to make soft pictures that could be rolled without cracking. This made it easier to fit film into small round containers, such as pencils. Abel then set up a shortwave radio so he could communicate directly with Moscow.

The Careful Spy

It is not easy to hide all the equipment a spy needs. So instead of hiding it, Abel used it as part of his cover story. He told his neighbors that he was a professional photographer and that his hobby was radios! His neighbors accepted Abel's story without question, and became good friends of his. They were all painters, with very little interest in politics. Apparently, they had no suspicions about the truth at all. One of them once walked in on Abel while he was receiving a radio message from Moscow. Abel nervously turned off his set, but the neighbor thought nothing of it. In fact, Abel later heard him explaining to another friend that he and "Emil" had been enjoying a broadcast from Russia!

Years later, when Abel had been captured, the F.B.I. was embarrassed to find a clue it had overlooked. One of the artists in Abel's building had painted a picture of his friend. On the day Abel's espionage career ended, the picture was hanging in the National Academy of Design. It was entitled "Emil Goldfus." "Emil's" spy radio was clearly shown in the background!

It wasn't only Abel's friends who believed his cover story. No one else was the least bit suspicious of him either. Considering how much illegal work he had to do, Abel was actually fairly safe from capture. New York City is such a large and busy place that it is easy to get lost in the crowd there. Even his agents knew nothing about their boss. To them, he was a faceless man known only as "Mark" who told them to pick up a message by drawing a chalk line on a subway wall. If a face-to-face meeting *was* needed for some reason, Abel showed up in a dark barroom with a hat pulled low on his face. The other agents never heard the names Emil Goldfus or Martin Collins, or knew the address of Abel's "spy shop" in Brooklyn.

A Fatal Mistake

Abel must have led a lonely life, but he was a dedicated professional. There was a job to be done for his country and he made sure to do it right. He spied successfully for several years and, because of all his precautions, he probably felt he would never be caught. And he would not have, if he had not made one fatal mistake.

In 1952, Abel began to feel overworked. He asked Moscow to send him an assistant. On October 21, 1952, Reino Hayhanen arrived from Finland. He was thirty-two years old, and a lieutenant in the KGB. Like Abel, Hayhanen had long ago been provided with a false identity — that of Eugene Nicolo Maki, an American who had lived for many years in Finland. Hayhanen came to America with another KGB agent who posed as his wife.

BE
CAREFUL
OF
RIDERS

The day after he arrived in New York, Hayhanen went to Central Park. As he had been instructed in Moscow, he looked for a sign on a horseback riding path saying "Be Careful of Riders." Near the sign was a fence. Hayhanen placed a red thumb tack in the fence. It meant: I have gotten here safely and am ready to work. His answer, left by Abel the next day, was a white thumb tack. This signal had also been arranged in Moscow. It meant: Go to the drop and pick up a message.

Hayhanen began to spy for Abel. Unfortunately, he was not very good at his job. He forgot some of the codes he was supposed to know and several of the photographic techniques. He missed some message pick-ups at Abel's drops, and sometimes even failed to obey orders. Abel became very angry with him. "Didn't they teach you anything in Moscow?" he once asked, sarcastically.

That's when Abel made the mistake that cost him his freedom. He was so good at his job that he couldn't stand to see someone else do it badly. So he took Hayhanen to his Brooklyn studio, to teach him to make microdots and soft film. In doing so, he broke his most important rule — he allowed an agent to see where he worked. Hayhanen still didn't know Abel's name, but now he knew his address.

The strain of being in a foreign country and working for such a strict boss began to upset Hayhanen. He started to do everything a spy should not. He drank heavily and had screaming fights, in public, with the agent who posed as his wife. He skipped even more of the errands Abel assigned him, and began to be careless about security.

Finally, Abel had had enough. He arranged for Hayhanen to be called back to Russia — where he would almost certainly be punished for his behavior. To avoid upsetting Hayhanen, Abel told him he was being sent back for a rest and a promotion. Hayhanen, however, was not fooled. He accepted the ticket Abel gave him on a ship named the *Liberty.* But when he arrived in France, he did not contact the Soviet agent assigned to him. Instead, he went to the American Embassy. "I am Reino Hayhanen, a KGB agent, and I want to give myself up," he told officials there.

His manner was so wild that the F.B.I., at first, was not sure whether to believe him or not. But Hayhanen soon proved that his story was true by decoding a message — the same message that Jimmy Bozart had found several years before. Hayhanen took the F.B.I. agents to Abel's Brooklyn studio. The agents staked-out the building until Hayhanen pointed out his boss. "That's Mark!" he cried excitedly, as Abel left the studio one day. The F.B.I. tailed Abel to his Manhattan hotel. There, on a hot morning in June, 1957, he was arrested. He was sentenced to thirty years in prison, but served only a small part of his term.

In 1960, an American pilot, named Francis Gary Powers, was flying a spy plane over the Soviet Union. He was on a secret mission for the United States when his plane was shot down. Powers was captured, convicted as a spy, and sent to jail. Eventually, the United States and the Soviet Union agreed to exchange prisoners. Abel returned to his homeland, where he received a hero's welcome and many medals. As far as anyone knows, the master Soviet spy of the twentieth century is living there still.

THE CULPER GANG

Jonas Hawkins was probably one of the most nervous spies in history. When delivering secret messages, it was not unusual for him to break out in a cold sweat and shake with fright. If an enemy soldier came anywhere near him, even innocently, Jonas immediately decided that he had been discovered. Sure that he was about to be searched, Jonas would step to the side of the road and stuff his secret papers into a sewer. Many important documents were washed away because of Jonas' nerves.

Jonas was part of one of our country's very first spy rings — the Culper gang. They received their name from Abraham Woodhull who used the name Samuel Culper when signing his secret notes to General George Washington. Like America in 1776, the Culpers were rough and unpolished. Abraham Woodhull, for example, was even more nervous than Jonas. When something went wrong with the spy ring, as it frequently did, Abraham took to his bed. He ran a fever, but he was actually sick with fright. Robert Townsend, Abraham's partner, did not even want to become a spy. He quit several times during the war, but was always persuaded to join again. Another Culper, known only as "Lady," spied even though everyone else in the gang told her to stop. The other spies were afraid for her safety, but she was not.

Lady should have been scared. It was the middle of the Revolutionary War, and the Culpers were living behind British lines. The British commander, General Clinton, had troops all over New York City and Long Island. They were constantly searching Americans for smuggled messages. And the penalty for spying, as the Culpers well knew, was death!

General George Washington was in Connecticut, desperate for news about British activities in New York. The Culpers were true American patriots. There was no real choice for them. They willingly risked their lives — and their peace of mind — to help the rebel cause.

Culper Sr. and Culper Jr.

Abraham Woodhull started the Culper ring when he began to collect information about British troop movements on Long Island. Since he lived in Setauket, which is located on the northern shore of Long Island, it was easy for him to send dispatches across Long Island Sound to General Washington. However, this was not enough. Washington needed more information than Woodhull alone could give him. He needed someone who lived in New York City, since that was where the British headquarters was located.

Abraham, who used the code name Samuel Culper, asked his friend Robert Townsend for help. Like Abraham, Robert had grown up on Long Island. His father owned a store. It would be simple, argued Abraham, for Robert to move to New York City and start a store there. No one would be suspicious if Robert were to travel frequently back and forth to Long Island.

But Robert protested. "I would like to help General Washington," he declared, "but I cannot be a spy." Robert was a Quaker. The Quaker religion does not allow fighting or participating in wars. To Robert, spying seemed to be a sneaky, dirty thing to do. He supported the American cause, but he did not feel he could spy for it. However, Abraham's arguments wore him down. Reluctantly, Robert agreed to become "Culper Junior" and collect information for General Washington.

He set up a business in New York City and joined the staff of a newspaper called the *Royal Gazette*. Since all the articles in the *Gazette* were strongly in favor of the British, no one suspected that Robert was really on the side of the Americans. Moreover, it was natural for a newspaper reporter to spend time gossiping with British officers to pick up leads for stories. Only in Robert's case, the stories were also going to George Washington!

Samuel Culper and Culper Junior made quite a pair. Robert's conscience sometimes bothered him and made him reluctant to search out information. At times, even after the information had been gathered, Abraham was too scared to travel with it! The addition of Austin Roe and Anna Strong made the Culper gang more efficient.

A mysterious agent named Lady completed the spy ring. No one has ever found out Lady's real name. All we know is that she was beautiful, and from a well-to-do family. It was Lady's job to go to all the society parties given by British officers. Her looks and charm were a great help to her. If a British officer missed a party, for example, Lady would act annoyed. "What was so important that you could not come and dance with me?" she would demand. Often the officer would explain, and his answer would soon be on its way to George Washington.

Invisible Ink

Since all the spies were in constant danger, it's no wonder that a new invention calmed Abraham's nerves a bit. Dr. James Jay, brother of our first justice of the Supreme Court, John Jay, worked out a formula for invisible ink. This ink, which the spies called "stain," looked like ordinary ink when it was first put on paper. But after a few moments, it faded from sight. The paper seemed to be completely blank! When another liquid, called a developer, was brushed on the page, the writing appeared again.

Unfortunately, the ingredients for "stain" were very hard to get. Jay could only find enough for one jar of ink. Washington himself kept the developer. That way, if one of the spies were captured, there would be no way their message could be developed and read.

Abraham was so excited about using the new stain that he immediately made a trip to see "Culper Junior." Robert told Abraham all his news, and Abraham went back to the rooming house where he was staying to write it down. But his nerves betrayed him again, and caused a serious setback for the Culper spy ring. As Abraham sat writing his message, the door suddenly flew open! Abraham jumped up, sure that he was about to be marched to the gallows. His hand swept over the table, knocking the precious jar to the floor. In dismay, the spy turned to face the intruders. They were two pretty girls — his sister Mary and a friend. "We came to surprise you," they giggled.

"You most certainly did," replied Abraham sadly, as he eyed the puddle of invisible ink spreading across the floor. Later that day, he rode home to Setauket. He was so upset that he went to bed with chills and fever.

The Secret Code

Until Dr. Jay could find the ingredients for more invisible ink, General Washington and his spies had to go back to writing ordinary letters. Unfortunately one of these was captured. In it, Washington mentioned "C____r Jr." who worked in New York and gave him "information respecting Long Island." The British now knew that there was a spy ring operating in New York and Long Island, so the Culper's work became doubly dangerous. To help keep their messages secret, one of Washington's officers set up a code.

It was the worst code imaginable — hard to write and easy to break. The most common words in the English language were listed, and each was given a number. The words were in alphabetical order. "The" was 628, "they" was 629, "there" was 630, and so forth. At the end of the list were people's names. Washington was to be called 711, and Lady 355; Abraham and Robert were 722 and 723.

The problem was that no one could remember all those numbers! To write a message, the code book was needed. Each spy was given one, but that was very dangerous. Just to be caught with such a book was enough evidence for hanging. It also took too long to write a message, since each word had to be looked up. On the other hand, the code could be broken with only a few hours study, since the words were in alphabetical order.

Robert realized all this immediately, and refused to use the code. However, Abraham loved it. He quickly wrote a letter to Washington. That letter was a perfect example of what *not* to do with a code. Part of it was in ordinary English. One line, for example, read as follows: "28 met 723 not far from 727 and received a 356." The English words give perfect clues to the meanings of the numbers. As if that weren't enough,

Abraham added a "P.S." at the end of the letter. The "P.S." explained what the numbers meant! Luckily, Abraham's message was never captured. Eventually the whole code was dropped, except for the numbers used for people's names.

Petticoats and Handkerchiefs

Jay finally found enough ingredients to make another bottle of stain. Robert used it this time, in very clever ways. He realized that a man carrying a blank sheet of paper would appear unusual; so he sent whole packages of blank paper to imaginary customers. One of the papers contained the secret message, but it looked like all the other sheets. To be even safer, Robert changed the position of the message each time. Sometimes it would be the 20th sheet, sometimes the 25th, and so forth. However, Abraham occasionally became confused and sent the wrong paper to Washington! Robert also wrote letters to his customers, being sure to pick those who strongly supported the British. The letters had wide spaces between the lines, and never reached the people to whom they were addressed. Robert had writen in the spaces with stain, and sent the letters across the Long Island Sound to the American's camp. At Washington's suggestion, the end papers of books and pamphlets were also used.

The spies had other schemes to help them avoid suspicion. Austin Roe seldom delivered his messages directly to Abraham. Instead, he buried them in a field near "Culper's" house. Later Abraham would go out for a stroll and retrieve the box. Then he would walk a little further and check Anna Strong's clothesline. Anna's husband had been arrested and imprisoned by the British. She had good reason to work for an American victory. Anna would do a wash. She would hang out a black petticoat, followed by white handkerchiefs. This was the code that told Abraham where the boat was waiting. Two handkerchiefs meant the second cove, three meant the third, and so forth. Abraham delivered the message to the boat and it was then taken across the Sound to Connecticut.

The French Fleet

The Culper's greatest success came in July, 1780. The Americans' spirit at that time was at its lowest point. George Washington and his troops had just spent a terrible winter. Cold, lack of food, and illness had claimed many lives. But with the arrival of summer, the Americans' hopes rose again. Washington knew that a fleet of French ships was coming to help him attack the British. Their help could turn the tide in favor of the Americans.

However, the French, like any troops after a long sea voyage, would be weak and disorganized when they arrived. They would need at least a few days to recover before they were able to fight. In order to help them, Washington had to know the minute the French landed. He also needed advance notice of the British plans. American spies in New England took care of the first part. They sent word immediately to General Washington when the French landed in Newport, Rhode Island; but it was up to the Culpers to find out what the British intended to do.

Robert began to hang around the docks in New York, pretending to buy goods for his store. However, his real mission was to keep an eye on the British fleet. When he saw them making preparations to sail, Robert became frantic. The British were obviously going to do something, but what? Were they planning to sail all the way to Newport, or would they make their stand closer to New York? Robert had to know, but no matter how hard he tried, he could not find out.

But Lady could. Robert knew that, but he was afraid to ask her. During the long months of spying for the American cause, Robert had fallen in love with Lady. He knew that she risked her life every time she began asking questions. He could not bear to see her in danger. Once he had even quit the Culper gang in an effort to make Lady quit too. But Lady refused. "If I stop going to British parties," she told Robert firmly, "the British will wonder why. I will be under even more suspicion than I am now. And if I am going to be at the parties anyway, I may as well find out what I can. You can't stop me."

Robert couldn't stop her then, and he couldn't now. Lady found out what Washington needed to know, and raced to Robert with the news. The British were going to Newport! The message passed through the usual Culper route, but faster than any message had ever gone before. Washington also acted quickly. His troops were not strong enough to help the French, so he tried a trick. He wrote a false message saying that the Americans were going to attack New York. He arranged for it to fall into British hands. British army officers at the tip of Long Island were frantic when they read the message. If the Americans attacked New York while the British ships were in Newport, the city might be captured. The British had already sailed, but the British officers on the Island had smoke signals sent up. "Go back, New York is being attacked," the signals said. British General Clinton immediately turned his fleet around and headed for home. How angry he must have been to find a peaceful city waiting for him!

Death Ship

Lady was successful that time, but her spying career was almost over. A few months after the French affair, some of Washington's officers learned of a plot to sell important information to the British. The buyer was Major Andre, a British officer who made his headquarters in New York. He had arranged to receive plans for the defense of West Point, an American Fort, from Benedict Arnold. Arnold was an American general who had gone over to the British side.

Before the sale could take place, Andre was caught by the Americans and hung. Arnold escaped into British territory. He was sure he had been betrayed by a spy, and he was determined to find out by whom. He began to question everyone in Andre's circle. Lady had nothing to do with Andre's death, but Arnold became suspicious of her anyway. He had her arrested.

Lady was sent to the *Jersey,* a prison boat in New York Harbor. The *Jersey* had a terrible but accurate nickname — death ship. A thousand people, all under suspicion and arrested by the British, were crowded together in the *Jersey's* hold. There were no toilets and very little food. The average prisoner lasted only three months.

Lady was questioned again and again about the Culper gang while on the *Jersey.* Perhaps she was even offered freedom in exchange for the names of her partners. One thing is certain: Lady said nothing at all. The other Culpers remained free. Weakened by her ordeal on the *Jersey,* Lady died. The only Culper who was not afraid, was the only one to die for her country. In spite of their fears, the other spies in the ring lived to see peace and victory come to the land they had served so well.

IS JAMES BOND DEAD?

Most modern spies give their masters very few worries. They work around the clock without getting tired, and they never ask for a vacation. Their loyalty need never be suspected — they harbor no thoughts of going over to the other side as a double agent. They never even ask for a pay raise. In fact, they are paid nothing at all! The most these present-day James Bonds ever need is a tightening of a bolt, a drop of oil here and there, and perhaps a new battery once in a while.

In other words, modern spies are usually machines. They come in many forms. Code-makers and code-breakers, for example, are now complex computers whose electronic brains work faster and better than the smartest humans. Instead of weak human ears, sensitive listening equipment picks up secret radio communications thousands of miles away. A spy who can steal documents, like Cicero, is no longer important when it is possible for machines in Washington and Moscow to record *all* the electronic messages of a foreign government, even if that government is on the other side of the world.

Intelligence agencies today also have mechanical "eyes" on other countries. High-flying spy planes, full of tremendously complex cameras, routinely pass over other nations to "see" what is going on. Even better are "spy-in-the-sky" satellites which survey large areas quickly. They fly so high that it is almost impossible to shoot them down or capture them. Yet, they are so sensitive that they can get recognizable pictures of objects only a few feet wide.

Does that mean that James Bond is gone forever? Definitely not. They may be fewer, but human spies will never be completely out-dated. No matter how mechanical the business of spying becomes, men and women are still needed to invent and operate the complex machinery. They perform all the *human* tasks that machines cannot. There will always be people who are convinced that their cause is right, and who will risk their lives to prove it. Just like Abel, Belle Boyd, and the Culper gang, they must use tricks and false identities to hide their real intentions.

So keep your eyes open. The orange juice carton that man on the park bench is holding may just contain a secret message. That innocent-looking radio in your neighbor's house might be a shortwave transmitter. In the world of real-life spies, anything is possible!

BEWARE OF
SPIES!